Contents

Star Light, Star Bright	4
The Sun	6
Skywatchers	8
A Cold New World	10
The Big Picture	12
Windows on Our Universe	14
Telescopic Technology	15
Calling Ground Control	20
Comets and Asteroids	22
Eye in the Sky	24
Working in Space	26
Space Adventurers	28
Glossary	30
Index	31
Research Starters	32

Features

Some people talk about the "man in the moon", but in this poem the moon is a woman with silver shoes! Find out more on page 5.

Do you think there are only nine planets in our solar system? Astronomers may have found another one. Read **Beyond Pluto** on page 11.

How can a telescope give us images of objects invisible to our eyes? Discover more in **Calling Ground Control** on page 20.

Stephen Hawking wrote a best-selling book explaining his theory on the history of the universe. Find out more in **Black Holes Revealed** on page 22.

Why can't people see black holes?
Visit **www.infosteps.co.uk**
for more about **OUTER SPACE**.

Star Light, Star Bright

Since ancient times people have been fascinated with the changing of day into night. When we look into space at night we can see countless stars. Most of these stars lie in millions of **galaxies** scattered across the **universe**. People have written poems and songs about the moon and the stars. Artists have tried to catch the magic of dawn, dusk and the night sky in their paintings.

As technology improves **astronomers** learn more about the stars, galaxies and the universe.

Vincent van Gogh's painting *Starry Night* depicts the night sky as a vibrant ever-changing universe.

WORD BUILDER

Slowly, silently, now the moon
Walks the night in her silver shoon;
This way, and that, she peers, and sees
Silver fruit upon silver trees;
One by one the casements catch
Her beams beneath the silvery thatch...

From the poem "Silver" by Walter de la Mare.

In this poem the poet describes the moon as if it were a woman wearing silver shoes, lighting all that she touches. When an animal or an object such as the moon is given human characteristics, it is called personification. Personification is often used in poetry.

The Sun

During the day we can see one star in the sky—the sun. The sun is a normal star like millions of others in our galaxy called the Milky Way. For Earth it is the most important object in the sky because its energy powers Earth's climate and supports life.

Many scientists think our solar system, consisting of the sun and nine planets, was formed about five billion years ago when a nearby star exploded. This caused a dense cloud of gas and dust known as a **nebula** to shrink in on itself. Gas collected in the centre of the nebula and became the sun. Over millions of years space dust and gases formed the planets that **orbit** the sun.

At night when the sun's light is gone from the sky we can see many stars. Scientists now know that some of these stars, like the sun, also have families of planets. These stars will live for billions of years.

Seeing the Sun

Telescopes can make images from invisible light waves. These images of the sun show invisible ultraviolet light waves at different layers of the sun's atmosphere.

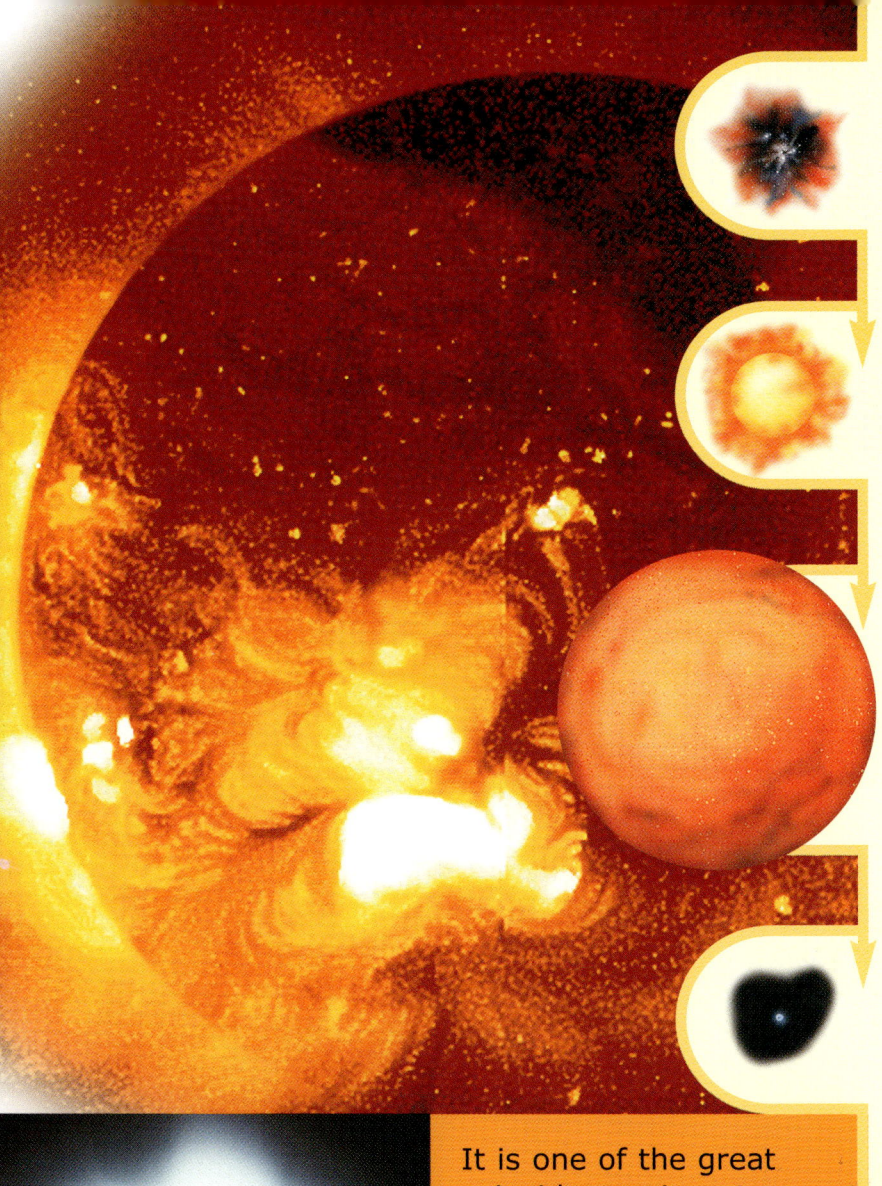

The Life Cycle of a Star

A star forms in the centre of a nebula.

In about 40 million years the star is fully formed. Like the sun it may have a system of planets.

After about 10 billion years the star's hydrogen fuel begins to run low. The star swells into a red giant.

Eventually the star explodes. The outer layers turn into a cloud of gas. The rest shrinks to the size of Earth and is called a hot white dwarf.

It is one of the great coincidences in nature that the sun is 400 times the size of Earth's moon and also lies 400 times further away than the moon. This explains why both objects look about the same size in our sky, occasionally resulting in spectacular **eclipses** casting shadows over large areas of Earth.

Skywatchers

For thousands of years people believed that Earth was the centre of the universe. In 1543 a Polish astronomer named Nicolaus Copernicus caused much anger and debate because he claimed that Earth and other planets travelled around the sun. When the first telescopes were built in the 1600s Galileo Galilei and others were able to prove the ideas of Copernicus and expand their view of the universe.

Much of what we know about the universe began with Galileo. He was the first person to study the universe using a telescope.

More powerful telescopes led to more discoveries. In 1781 William Herschel looked through his telescope and found the planet Uranus. Until then, astronomers had only known about six planets: Mercury, Venus, Earth, Mars, Jupiter and Saturn.

The eighth planet, Neptune, was first sighted in 1846 after astronomers noticed that Uranus wasn't moving as they had predicted. They guessed there must be another planet further out and they were able to calculate exactly where to find Neptune in the sky.

Voyager 2

In 1989 *Voyager 2* made a flyby of Neptune. It sent vast amounts of information back to Earth. Computer-generated images were produced from this information.

A Cold New World

The very small icy planet Pluto was discovered by Clyde Tombaugh in 1930 after a long search. Pluto seems to be different from the other planets. It has an irregular orbit around the sun. For most of Pluto's long year the surface of the planet is frozen. As it moves closer to the sun some of the surface materials turn from solids into gases.

Scientists had thought that the discovery of Pluto would explain the irregular orbits of both Neptune and Uranus. However, Pluto was far too small to have such an effect on their orbits. The search for other planets and their moons continues.

Pluto is not only smaller than all the other planets, it is also smaller than some of the planets' moons. Shown here to scale (from left to right): Pluto, Earth's moon and Ganymede, one of Jupiter's 16 known moons.

Astronomy Today

October 7, 2002

Beyond Pluto

A large object has been found over one billion kilometres beyond Pluto. Quaoar (pronounced KWAH-whar) moves around the sun every 288 years in a nearly perfect circle. Its diameter is almost 1,300 kilometres and is about half the size of Pluto.

An artist's impression of Quaoar

Quaoar, like Pluto, lies in the Kuiper Belt, a mass of objects made of ice and rock. The discovery of Quaoar fits in with the expectation of astronomers that there are other large objects like Pluto. But is Quaoar a planet? Some astronomers say it has a different make-up and is too small to be considered a planet.

Other astronomers also say Pluto is not really a planet. They think it should be known as the largest Kuiper Belt Object (KBO) yet found. It is thought there are still more large KBOs to be discovered.

Scientists plan to launch a spacecraft in 2006. It would fly past Pluto and its moon Charon as early as 2015 and it would pass many objects in the Kuiper Belt by 2026. It is hoped the long journey will help answer basic questions about the geology, interior make-up and atmospheres of these objects.

The Big Picture

We think Earth is a big place! To try visualizing the vastness of the universe is a real challenge. Today new theories and new technology have led to great leaps in our understanding of space. We now know that the universe is much larger than our solar system. However, there is still a lot we don't know.

Solar system

Earth

Most of what we see when we look into the night sky is just a very small part of the Milky Way galaxy—and the Milky Way is just one among many billions of galaxies.

Windows on Our Universe

On a clear dark night we can look into the sky speckled with stars. Some stars are bright and look close while others appear faint and far away. The moon is usually visible sometime during the night and sometimes up to five planets are also visible. The universe is so big that beams of light from the most distant parts of space take billions of years to reach us. When we look into the sky we are looking back in time.

Today when we use binoculars we can see as much as Galileo saw through his simple telescope in 1609. Telescopes at observatories, planetariums and science centres reveal even more of the sky's secrets. Telescopes collect the light coming from distant objects and magnify it, allowing us to see planets, stars and galaxies as if they were much closer.

This robotic machine is called a rover. It is designed to take samples from the surface of Mars. Scientists are able to study the information collected by the rover. They hope to learn more about the history of the planet's climate and discover any evidence of water and life.

Telescopic Technology

In 1671 Sir Isaac Newton built the first reflecting telescope that used a mirror to collect light. Today most telescopes used by astronomers in observatories are reflectors like Newton's invention. They are, however, much larger. The telescopes have very large mirrors that can gather a lot of light. This lets astronomers see further into space. Some telescopes have mirrors as wide as houses.

Astronomers continue to make discoveries as telescopes become more powerful. In 2002 an international team of astronomers working at the Anglo-Australian Telescope near Coonabarabran, Australia announced the discovery of the 102nd planet outside our solar system. The new planet is similar in size to Jupiter and orbits the star Tau 1 Gruis about 100 **light years** away.

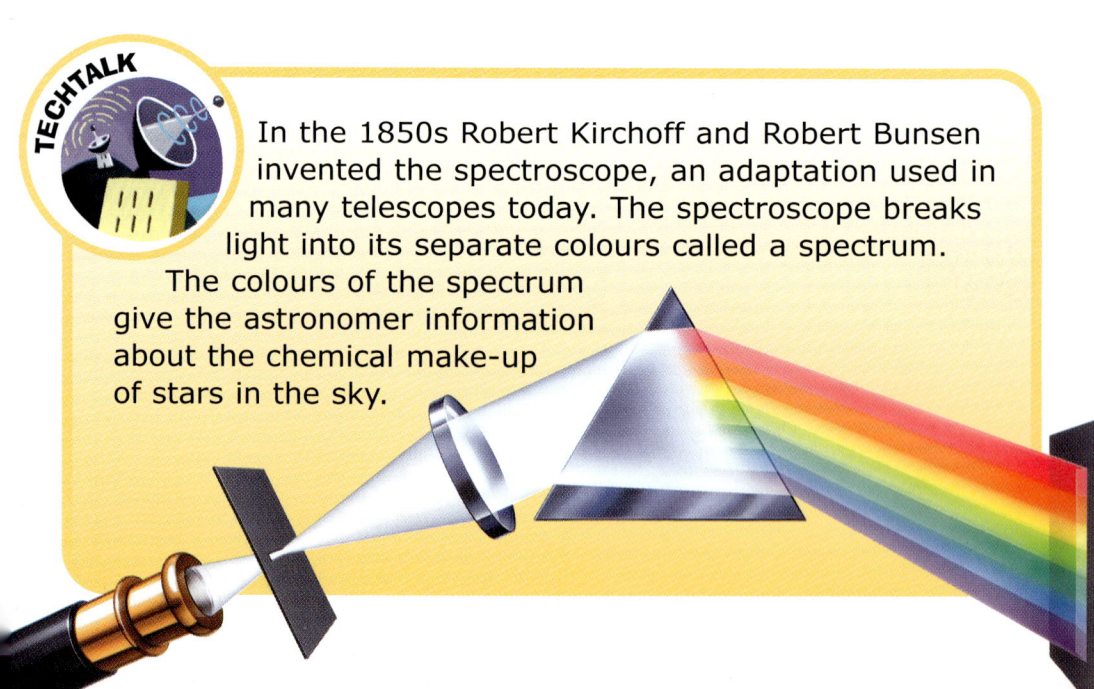

TECHTALK

In the 1850s Robert Kirchoff and Robert Bunsen invented the spectroscope, an adaptation used in many telescopes today. The spectroscope breaks light into its separate colours called a spectrum. The colours of the spectrum give the astronomer information about the chemical make-up of stars in the sky.

Exploring Space

Since the late 1950s space has been explored by many types of spacecraft, giving us a wealth of knowledge about our solar system and beyond.

1957 — The first artificial satellite *Sputnik* is sent into space.

1959 — *Luna 2* is the first rocket to reach the moon.

Viewing room

Dome

Control room

Many astronomers believe that between 13 billion and 15 billion years ago all matter and energy were concentrated in a single point. They believe that there was a tremendous explosion that created gases such as helium and hydrogen. Over several billion years **gravity** caused the clouds of gases to collapse, forming the planets, stars and galaxies that we see today. Astronomers call this theory the **big bang theory**. The universe has continued to expand since the big bang.

Milky Way galaxy

The Milky Way and beyond

TECHTALK

Calling Ground Control

Most of us think of telescopes as being used only with human eyes. In the 1970s and 1980s the first small telescopes were launched into space. These telescopes observe different wavelengths of the **electromagnetic spectrum** that are blocked or changed by Earth's atmosphere. The advantage of the space telescopes is that they can produce pictures showing much finer details than an Earth-based telescope.

The Hubble Telescope was launched in 1990. It's about the size of a school bus and orbits Earth every 97 minutes taking the sharpest pictures of stars and galaxies ever seen. It sends these spectacular pictures by radio to astronomers back on the ground. Space telescopes have discovered exploding galaxies and **black holes** never before observed.

The Hubble Telescope peered across the Milky Way galaxy to find newborn stars emerging from nebula many thousands of light years away.

Cone Nebula

"Rotten Egg" Nebula

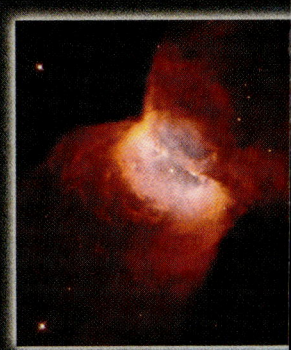
Papillon ("Butterfly") Nebula

- **1961** — Yuri Gagarin is the first human in space.
- **1969** — Neil Armstrong and Buzz Aldrin, on *Apollo 11*, become the first humans to walk on the moon.
- **1977–89** — *Voyager 1* and *2* spacecraft observe Jupiter, Saturn, Uranus and Neptune.
- **1991–2000** — Compton Gamma-Ray Observatory searches distant space.

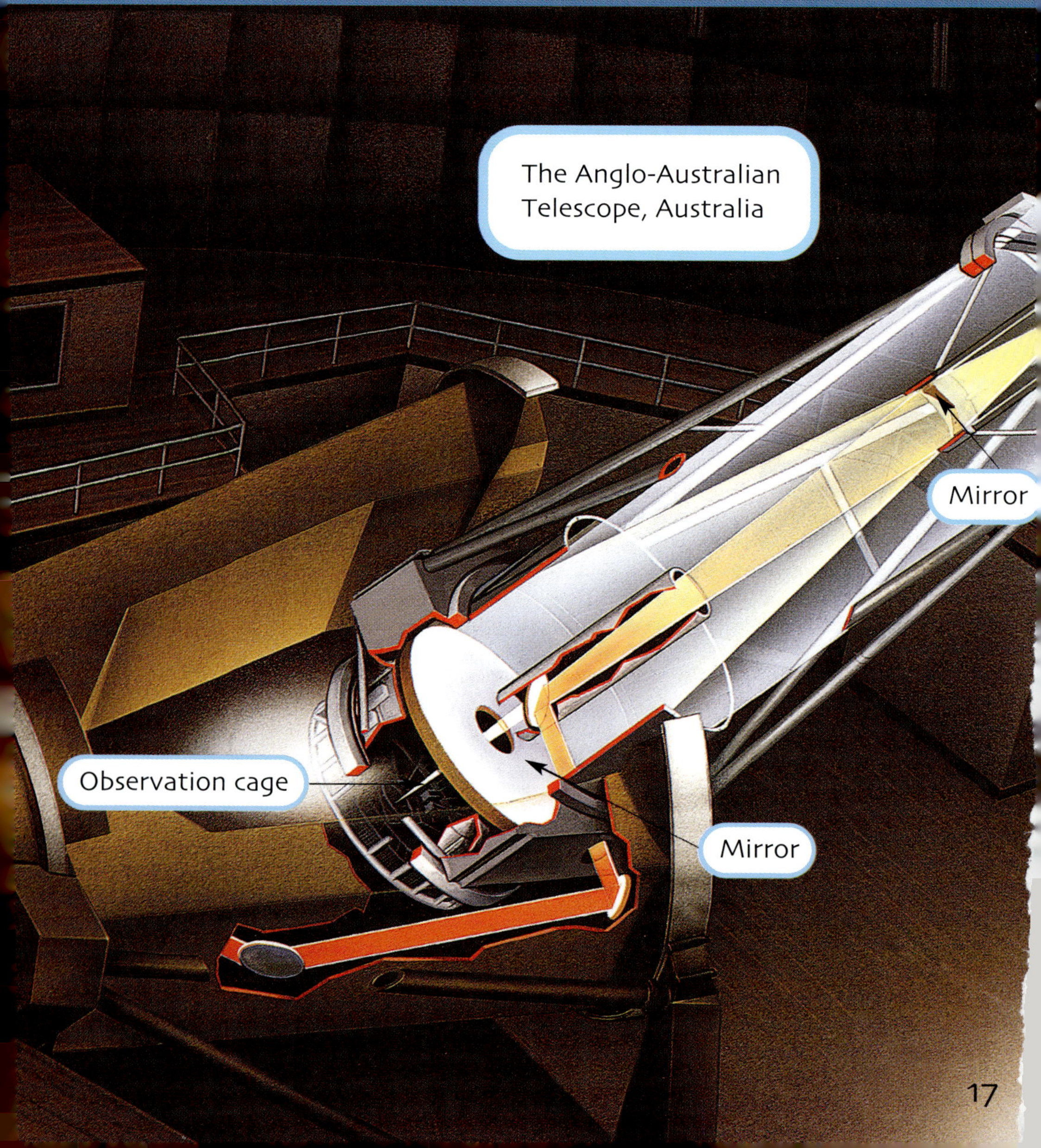

The Anglo-Australian Telescope, Australia

Mirror

Observation cage

Mirror

1998
The International Space Station is started.

2003
Space missions are launched to seek signs of life on Mars.

Windows on Our Universe continued

Astronomers continue to launch satellites and probes to explore outer space.

Incoming starlight

IN FOCUS

The Parkes Telescope in Australia is a radio telescope. On July 20, 1969 the world watched the *Apollo 11* television pictures of the first human footsteps on the moon. The images came from radio signals received by the Parkes Telescope. These signals were relayed to a worldwide audience of 600 million people.

A movie *The Dish* (starring from left, Tom Long, Patrick Warburton and Sam Neill) later portrayed the role of the telescope during the moon landing.

In 1970 the telescope played a vital role in tracking the crippled *Apollo 13* spacecraft. This effort resulted in the crew's safe return to Earth.

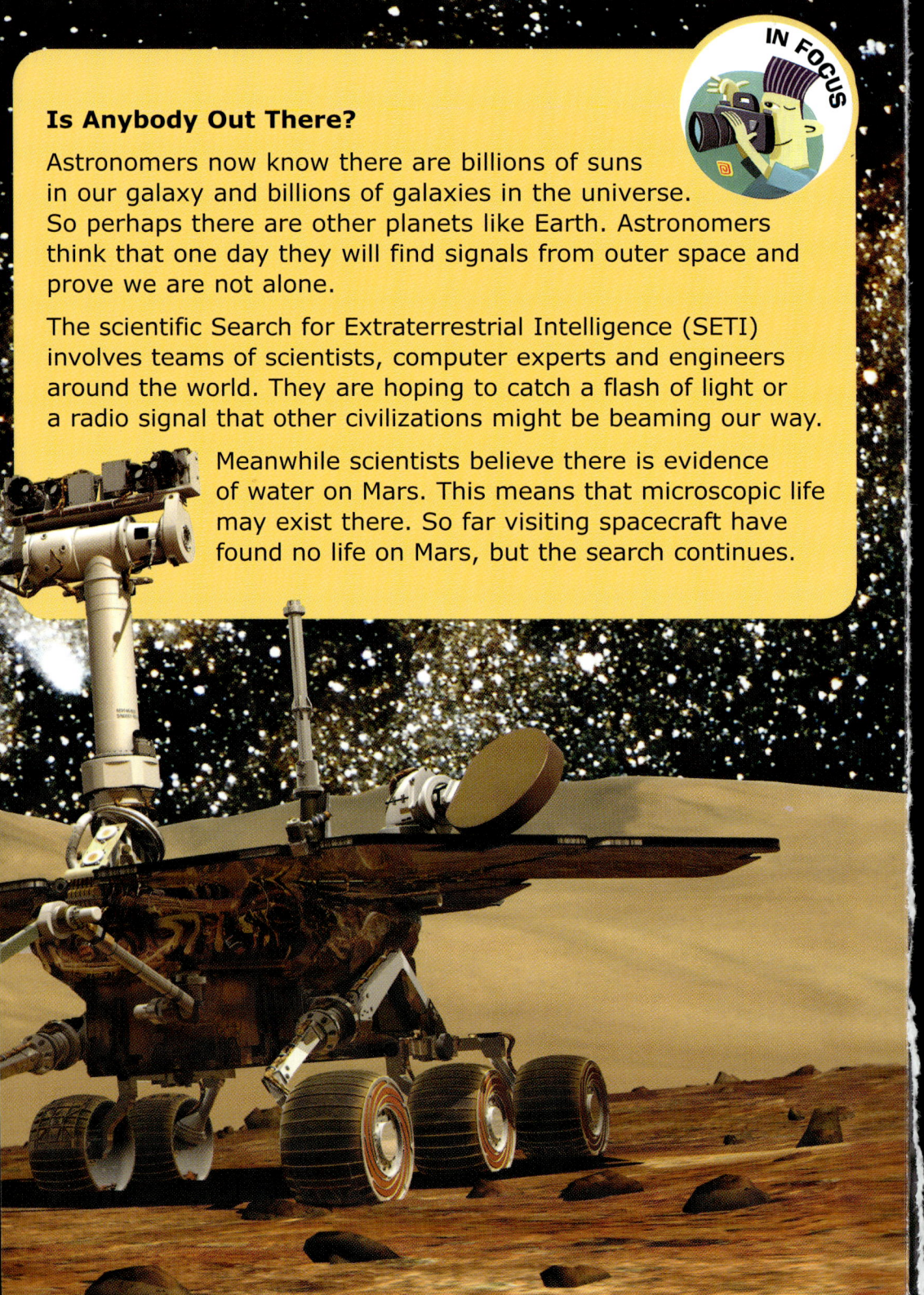

Is Anybody Out There?

Astronomers now know there are billions of suns in our galaxy and billions of galaxies in the universe. So perhaps there are other planets like Earth. Astronomers think that one day they will find signals from outer space and prove we are not alone.

The scientific Search for Extraterrestrial Intelligence (SETI) involves teams of scientists, computer experts and engineers around the world. They are hoping to catch a flash of light or a radio signal that other civilizations might be beaming our way.

Meanwhile scientists believe there is evidence of water on Mars. This means that microscopic life may exist there. So far visiting spacecraft have found no life on Mars, but the search continues.

Comets and Asteroids

Comets are like dirty snowballs of frozen ice and rock that sweep through the solar system. Most comets stay deep in space beyond Pluto. Sometimes a comet falls into an orbit that takes it towards the sun. As the comet gets closer to the sun's warmth, it forms gas and dust tails that can stretch for many millions of kilometres. Some comets travel close to Earth and can be seen in the sky.

The smallest flying objects in our solar system are asteroids and meteoroids. Astronomers think asteroids are lumps of rock and metal left over from the early days of the solar system. Meteoroids are fragments of asteroids and comets and are usually thumb-sized or smaller. Thousands of meteoroids collide with Earth every day.

Black Holes Revealed

Stephen Hawking is a British scientist who is best known for his theories about black holes. Hawking believes that black holes cause the enormous jets of hot gas and energy that astronomers have seen shooting from some galaxies. Hawking has explained his thinking about space in a book called *A Brief History of Time: From the Big Bang to Black Holes*.

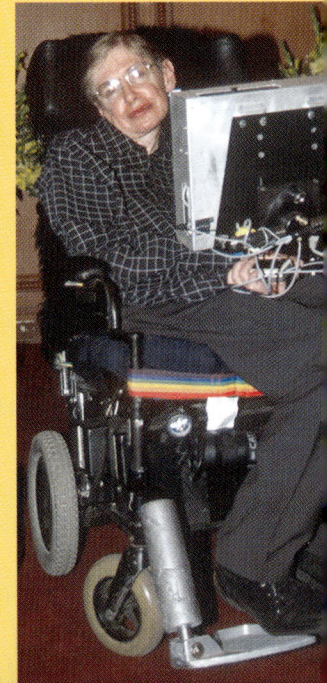

Occasionally large meteoroids fall through the atmosphere and crash to the ground. They are called meteorites when they reach Earth's surface. This meteorite on display in a museum is almost as big as a baby elephant.

Why can't people see black holes?
Visit **www.infosteps.co.uk**
for more about **OUTER SPACE**.

Eye in the Sky

Today many different artificial objects orbit Earth along with the Hubble Telescope. Only some of these satellites are looking into the unknown universe. Others are looking down on Earth. Many of these satellites are used to forecast the weather and relay telephone calls, Internet services and television programmes around the world.

Some satellites take photographs and measurements with their cameras and instruments. Satellites can assist in the navigation of ships or aircraft and monitor crops or other resources.

A satellite took this photograph of North America at night. It shows the glowing lights of the cities. Some people call this "light pollution".

A communication satellite, or comsat, works like a mirror in the sky. It receives radio signals beamed up from Earth and sends them back to a different place on Earth.

A low-flying satellite can dip down as low as 120 kilometres from Earth to take close-up photographs of our planet. Its cameras can see details of an area as small as 5 centimetres across.

Some satellites are called "spy satellites". They are used by the military to detect the launch of missiles and to follow the movements of ships at sea and military equipment on the ground.

Weather satellites carry heat-sensitive cameras that study weather patterns over large areas.

Working in Space

Many people dream of becoming an astronaut, but only a few are selected for training. To become an astronaut you must be very fit. You also need to have studied engineering, science or mathematics at university.

Dr Roberta Bondar

Working in the Spacelab

Floating on the Job

An interview with Canadian scientist and photographer Dr Roberta Bondar who was selected for astronaut training in 1983.

Q. How many times have you been in space?
A. I've been on one space mission. It was on the space shuttle *Discovery* during an eight-day mission in January 1992.

Q. What did you do in space?
A. I was performing scientific experiments in the Spacelab and on the mid-deck of the shuttle. I also took many photographs of Earth.

Q. What was the shuttle launch like?
A. For the first two minutes it was very exciting, noisy and shaky. Then the solid rocket boosters dropped off so it became smoother, but it felt like the back of my seat was being pushed in from all the power of the engines. The shuttle went from standing still on the launch pad to travelling at more than 27,000 kilometres per hour in just over 8 minutes.

Q. Was it fun floating in space?
A. It was a lot of fun. Moving around inside the shuttle was very easy. While I was in the Spacelab I hooked my feet into restraints on the wall to stop floating away from my work.

The crew

Space Adventurers

Space camps offer young people the chance to experience first-hand what it's like to be an astronaut. Participants find out more than how it feels to be weightless. They sometimes also learn how to eat, sleep and shower space-style.

Over five days a young space-camp astronaut will watch movies about space, build and launch a rocket and learn about space exploration in the past, the present and the future. The most popular activities are often with the **simulators**. These machines imitate the feeling of a rocket take-off, walking on the moon and zero gravity.

Space suits and helmets are really heavy. You wouldn't be able to get anywhere quickly in one of these suits!

Working in Space continued

WORD BUILDER

People who fly on American space missions are called astronauts. The word *astronaut* comes from two Greek words, *astron* and *naute*, meaning "star voyager". Russians who fly into space are called *cosmonauts*, meaning "voyagers into the cosmos". Today astronauts and cosmonauts fly together on space missions.

This is your commander speaking. Countdown has started. Fasten your seatbelts and prepare for lift off!

Glossary

astronomer – a scientist who studies the solar system, galaxies and the universe

big bang theory – the theory that the universe was formed as a result of a massive expansion of matter and energy

black hole – an object so dense and with such powerful gravity that no light can escape from it

eclipse – when one object passes in front of another blocking or dimming the other object's light

electromagnetic spectrum – the full range of radiation produced by nature from the longest radio waves to the shortest gamma rays

galaxy – a large cluster of billions of stars and clouds of gas and dust all held together by gravity

gravity – a force that pulls objects towards each other

light year – the distance a beam of light travels through space in one year. One light year is about 9,600 billion kilometres.

nebula – a dense cloud of dusty gas where new stars and planets form

orbit – the invisible curved path followed by one object such as Earth around another object such as the sun. The orbit is controlled by the gravity pull of the larger object.

simulator – a machine that imitates the conditions of a real situation

universe – everything that exists scattered through space

Index

Anglo-Australian Telescope	15–18
artificial satellites	16–18, 24–25
astronomers	
Bunsen, Robert	15
Copernicus, Nicolaus	8
Galilei, Galileo	8, 14
Hawking, Stephen	22
Herschel, William	9
Kirchoff, Robert	15
Newton, Sir Isaac	15
Tombaugh, Clyde	10
big bang theory	13
black holes	20, 22
Bondar, Dr Roberta	26–27
eclipses	7
Hubble Telescope	20–21, 24
Milky Way galaxy	6, 12–13, 20
nebulas	6–7, 20–21
Parkes Telescope	18
Quaoar	11
Search for Extraterrestrial Intelligence (SETI)	19
spectroscopes	15
Tau 1 Gruis	15

Research Starters

1 Most of our known planets have companion satellites called moons. Earth has one moon while Saturn has the most with eighteen. Some planets don't have any moons. Which ones are they? Find out how many moons orbit each of the remaining planets.

2 The further away a planet is from the sun the longer it takes to orbit. Earth takes one year or 365.25 days to orbit the sun. Find out how long it takes the other planets to orbit the sun.

3 Stars are formed and live for billions of years. Some then shrink to become hot white dwarf stars that will shine for billions more years. Others become supernovas. Find out more about the life cycle of stars, white dwarf stars and supernovas.

4 The planets near the sun are rocky while planets further away from the sun are mostly gas. Find out why.